Make Your Own

Water Balloon Launcher

Julia Garstecki and Stephanie Derkovitz

BLACK
RABBIT
BOOKS

Hi Jinx is published by Black Rabbit Books
P.O. Box 3263, Mankato, Minnesota, 56002.
www.blackrabbitbooks.com
Copyright © 2020 Black Rabbit Books

Marysa Storm, editor; Michael Sellner, designer;
Omay Ayres, photo researcher

Names: Garstecki, Julia, author. | Derkovitz, Stephanie, author.
Title: Make your own water balloon launcher / by Julia Garstecki and
Stephanie Derkovitz.
Description: Mankato, Minnesota : Black Rabbit Books, [2020] | Series:
Hi Jinx. Make your own fun | Includes bibliographical references and index.
Identifiers: LCCN 2018034736 (print) | LCCN 2018037240 (ebook) |
ISBN 9781680729443 (e-book) | ISBN 9781680729382 (library binding) |
ISBN 9781644660690 (paperback)
Subjects: LCSH: Toy making–Juvenile literature. | Balloons–Experiments–
Juvenile literature. | Catapult–Juvenile literature.
Classification: LCC TT174 (ebook) | LCC TT174 .G37 2020 (print) |
DDC 745.592–dc23
LC record available at https://lccn.loc.gov/2018034736

Printed in China. 1/19

Image Credits

Black Rabbit Books: Michael Sellner, 6 (launcher), 7 (washers, funnel,
tubing, rope), 8 (funnels), 10 (step), 10–11 (step), 11 (step), 12 (washer),
12–13, 14–15, 16 (launcher), 16–17 (launcher), 21 (launcher); Science
Source: Peter Menzel, 20 (btm); Shutterstock: Alena Kozlova, 4–5
(grass), 16 (grass), 18–19 (grass); Angeliki Vel, 4 (sun); Arcady, 7
(sticky note); Bunphot Kliaphuangphit, 7 (drill bit); Duplass,
2–3; Galyna G, 11 (bkgd); Jourdan Laik, 7 (Sharpie); kolopach,
Cover (water), 4–5 (water), 18–19 (water); Maria Ferencova,
1; Memo Angeles, Cover (kids), 4 (boy), 5 (kids), 6 (kid),
8 (hands), 16 (kids, hand), 17 (kid), 18 (kids), 19
(kids), 21 (kid); mohinimurti, Back Cover (bkgd), 4
(bkgd); MSSA, 16 (tree bkgd); Nosopyrik, 7 (ruler);
opicobello, 13, 14; Pasko Maksim, Back Cover
(tear), 19 (tear), 23 (top), 24; pitju, 6 (page curl),
15 (page curl), 21 (page curl); Rasdi Abdul
Rahman, 8 (Sharpie); Ron Dale, 5 (marker
stroke), 6 (marker stroke), 9, 16 (marker
stroke), 19 (marker stroke), 20 (marker
stroke); timquo, 7 (balloons), 23 (btm);
totallypic, 10 (arrow), 11 (arrow), 12
(arrow); Vectomart, Cover (balloon), 4–5
(balloon), 18–19 (balloon), wk1003mike,
7 (drill) Every effort has been made to
contact copyright holders for material
reproduced in this book. Any omissions
will be rectified in subsequent printings
if notice is given to the publisher.

Contents

CHAPTER 1

Get Ready for
Some Fun!. 5

CHAPTER 2

Let's Build!. 6

CHAPTER 3

Get in on the Hi Jinx. .20

Other Resources. 22

Chapter 1
Get Ready for Some Fun!

Nobody likes being too hot during the summer. Having nothing to do is no good either. But don't worry! This book has the **solution** to both problems. It teaches you how to make your own water balloon launcher. It's perfect for cooling down and having a great time!

Chapter 2
Let's Build!

Building a water balloon launcher is easy. Just gather a few items. Then get to work. Some steps might be harder than others. But don't worry if something doesn't work right away. Just experiment until it does. And, most importantly, remember to have fun!

What You'll Need

plenty of filled water balloons

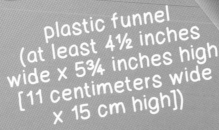

plastic funnel (at least 4½ inches wide × 5¾ inches high [11 centimeters wide × 15 cm high])

10 feet (3 meters) of ½-inch (1-cm) diameter elastic tubing

about 16 inches (41 cm) of thin rope (Any kind will work!)

marker

9/32 drill bit

2 1-inch (2.5-cm) washers

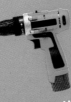

drill

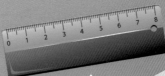

ruler

a **responsible** adult to help you

friends (It will take three people to use the launcher.)

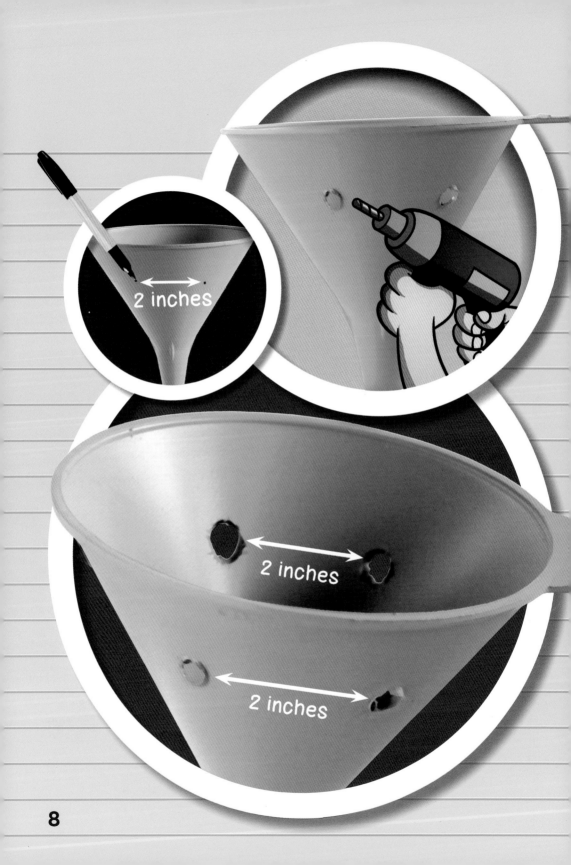

2 inches

2 inches

2 inches

Prepare the Funnel

1 On the funnel's outside, make a mark beneath the rim. Measure about 2 inches (5 cm) from the first mark. Make another mark.

2 Have your adult drill holes at the marks from Step 1.

3 Repeat Steps 1 and 2 on the **opposite** side of the funnel. The new holes should be directly across from the first two.

HINT

Make sure the holes are wider than the elastic tubing.

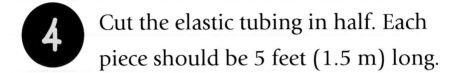

4 Cut the elastic tubing in half. Each piece should be 5 feet (1.5 m) long.

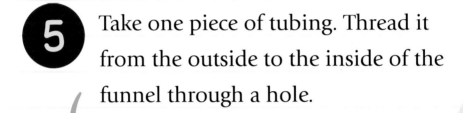

5 Take one piece of tubing. Thread it from the outside to the inside of the funnel through a hole.

6 Pull the tubing through the other hole on the same side. Both ends of the tubing should be outside of the funnel.

7 Make sure there is an equal amount of tubing on each side.

8 Grab the second piece of tubing. Repeat Steps 5 through 7 on the funnel's other side.

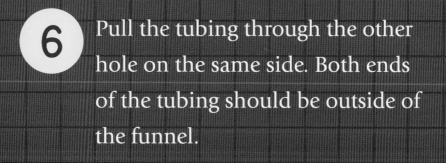

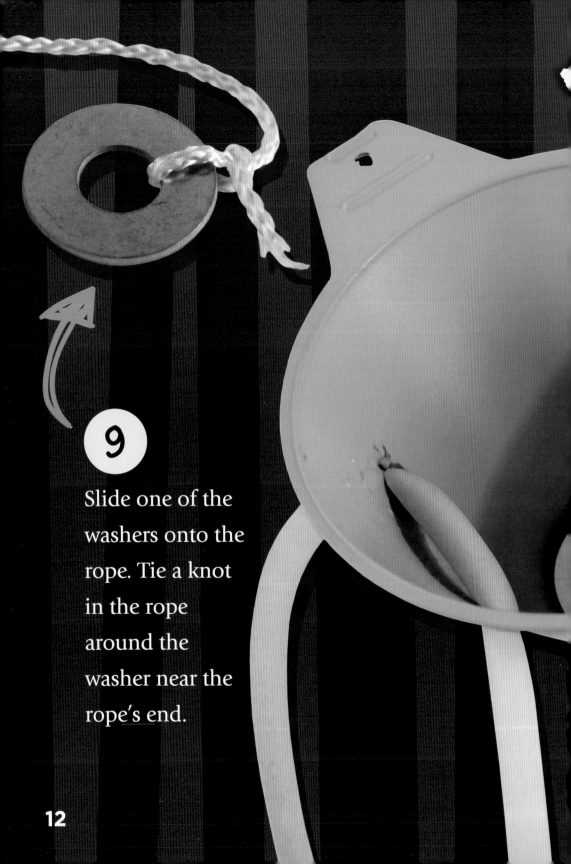

9

Slide one of the washers onto the rope. Tie a knot in the rope around the washer near the rope's end.

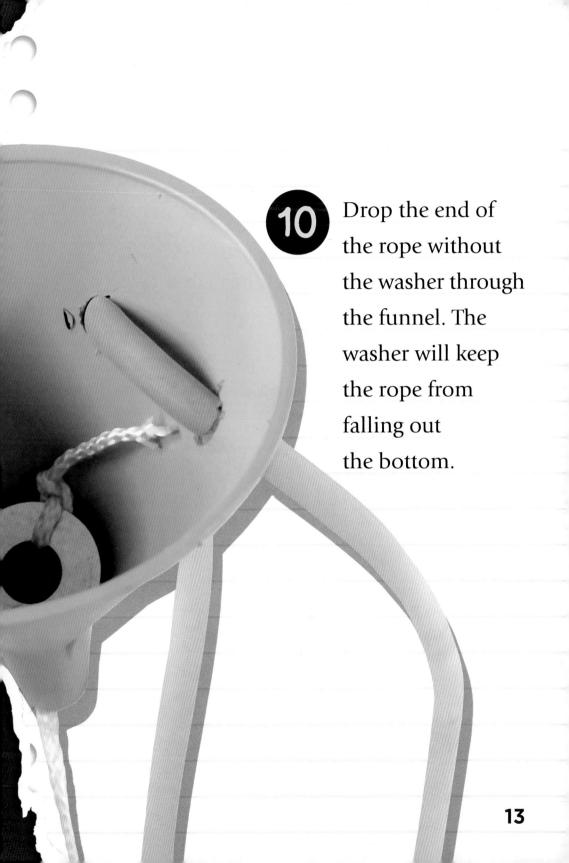

10 Drop the end of the rope without the washer through the funnel. The washer will keep the rope from falling out the bottom.

11 Thread the end of rope sticking out of the funnel through the other washer.

12 Tie a knot around the second washer near the end of the rope. You'll grab this washer when it's time to launch.

 Choose your target wisely. It's not nice to launch balloons at people or their property.

Prepare to Launch

1 Stand in a line with your friends. One person will hold the elastic tubing on each side of the funnel. Another person should hold the rope beneath the funnel.

2 Face an open space.

3 The people holding the elastic should step forward until the tubing is tight.

4 The person holding the rope should take a few steps back. He or she should also bend down.

5 Have the person holding the rope put a water balloon in the funnel. This step might be tricky at first. Just keep trying. Practice makes perfect!

6 Once the launcher is loaded, the middle person can release the rope. The balloon will fly through the sky.

Chapter 3
Get in on the
Hi Jinx

Balloons are a blast to play with. But they can be used for more than just fun. Balloons are often used in science. Weather balloons are used to gather information about Earth's **atmosphere**. They check wind, temperature, and **humidity**. They help weather people give better **forecasts**. Maybe someday you'll send weather balloons into the air.

Take It One Step More

1. Try pulling the funnel back into different positions. How does that change how the balloons fly?

2. What happens if the people holding the elastic move farther apart?

3. Try making this launcher with a larger funnel. How does a larger funnel change how your balloons fly?

GLOSSARY

atmosphere (AT-muhs-feer)—the gases that surround a planet

forecast (FAWR-kast)—a statement about what someone thinks is going to happen in the future

humidity (hyoo-MID-i-tee)—the amount of moisture in the air

opposite (AH-puh-set)—being in a position to oppose or cancel out

responsible (ri-SPON-suh-buhl)— able to be trusted to do what is right or to do things that are expected or required

solution (suh-LOO-shuhn)—the answer to a problem

BOOKS

Gaertner, Meg. *Make a Catapult.* Make Your Own: Make It Go! Chicago: Norwood House Press, 2018.

Hall, Kevin. *10 Great Makerspace Projects Using Math.* Using Makerspaces for School Projects. New York: Rosen Publishing, 2018.

Holzweiss, Kristina A. *Amazing Makerspace DIY Movers.* A True Book. New York: Children's Press, 2018.

WEBSITES

Largest Water Balloon Fight
www.guinnessworldrecords.com/world-records/largest-water-balloon-fight

Water Balloon
content.time.com/time/specials/packages/article/0,28804,2049243_2048654_2049039,00.html

Water Balloon Launcher
www.instructables.com/id/Water-Balloon-Launcher/

Don't be afraid to ask your adult for help. Some steps can be tricky.

No drill? No problem! Just use a large Phillips screwdriver to make holes in the funnel.

The friends holding the tubing should use both hands. Using both hands will help steady the launcher.